PRAYER
4
THE
BELIEVER

STUDIO
OF BOOKS
THE SPACE FOR YOUR MESSAGE

Studio of Books LLC
5900 Balcones Drive Suite 100
Austin, Texas 78731
www.studioofbooks.org
Hotline: (254) 800-1183

Ordering Information:
Special discounts are available on quantity purchases by corporations, associations, and others. For details, contact the publisher at the address above.

Printed in the United States of America.

ISBN-13: Paperback   978-1-964928-04-3
                eBook   978-1-964928-05-0

CONTENTS

TOPIC ONE

INTRODUCTION TO PRAYER

Amplified Bible

Genesis 1:26.

"Then God said, 'Let Us [Father, Son, Holy Spirit] make man in Our image, according to Our likeness [not physical, but a spiritual personality and moral likeness]; and let them have complete authority over…'"

Man and woman; was created to communicate with our heavenly Father, Son [The Word], and Holy Spirit. Prayer is the desirable instrument used to accomplish our communication. Due to the fall of man, we must become born again to have all rights and privileges available producing a personal relationship with our Father, Son, and Holy Spirit.

Scripture is filled with characters praying and calling on God for numerous reasons. We will look into some of the circumstances where pray, prayer and praying is recorded and see, according to scripture, what is involved when we pray, have prayer, and while we are praying.

The following examples demonstrate how we engage in conversation with an intended goal. The length and passion of the conversation is determined by the prompting of the conversation; *it is the same with prayer.* The components of conversation correlates to prayer.

1

CONVERSATION #1

A nervous thirteen-year old daughter is trying out tomorrow for the school Choir. Her mother follows her into the daughter's bedroom and they sit on the bed discussing what she will wear to school tomorrow. Thirty minutes later, the conversation ends.

CONVERSATION #2

Just before bedtime a thirteen-year old son stands in the doorway of his dad's room and tells him he is trying-out tomorrow for the football team. Dad tells his son to do his best and everything will be alright. After that brief conversation, both say "goodnight."

Just as each parent knows the components of their child's emotions, so it is with our heavenly Father. He listens and hears our conversations. Each word we utter has emotion attached and Our heavenly Father knows the intent of every word spoken. He knows His child.

Laying A Foundation

Before we plunge into pray, prayer and praying let us take a look into the realm of the spirit and lay the foundation with understanding.

Genesis 1: 27

"So God created man in His own image, in the image of God He created him; male and female created He them."

Genesis 2: 7 [KJV]

" And the LORD God formed man of the dust of the ground, and breathed into his nostrils the breath of life; and man became a living soul."

Genesis 2: 16,17

"And the LORD God commanded the man, saying, 'Of every tree of the garden you may eat freely; [17] but of the tree of the knowledge of good and evil you shall not eat, for in the day you eat of it you shall surely die.'"

Genesis 3: 4-7

" Then the serpent said to the woman, 'You shall not surely die. [5] For God knows that in the day you eat of it your eyes will be opened, and you will be like God, knowing good and evil.' [6] So when the woman saw that the tree was good for food, that it was pleasant for the eyes, and a tree desirable to make one wise, she took of its fruit and ate. She also gave to her husband with her, and he ate. [7] Then the eyes of both of them were opened, and they knew that they were naked; and they sewed fig leaves together and made themselves coverings."

We observe Adam and Eve in their wholeness before dying spiritually. Their relationship with the LORD was unblemished. Adam and Eve could hear very clear the move of God. Adam and Eve were alive spiritually and walked in the presence of God without struggle.

Gen. 2:8

"And they heard the sound of the Lord God walking in the garden in the cool of the day, and Adam and his wife hid themselves from the presence of the Lord God among the trees of the garden."

Eating the fruit of the knowledge of good and evil caused all of mankind to be born into sin. We must now become "Born Again" of the spirit and walk in the presence of God then are we able to hear with clarity the move of God. When this wonderful transformation happens, we are now capable of living and functioning in two realms, natural and spiritual.

Just as we develop gradually naturally; we also develop gradually to the life of the spiritual realm. Studying and meditating The Word causes us to grow in understanding. Learning how to handle trials and testing's, [life] in accordance with The Word is how we gain spiritual maturity.

Jesus told us over and over, "The kingdom of heaven is like... The kingdom of God is likened unto..." When we accept Christ as our savior He lives in us. Holy Spirit takes residence in us. When we, the born of the spirit pray, especially specific prayers that line up with The Word, we are able to experience Holy Spirit give life to The Word!

Being a born-again believer **"qualifies"** us through prayer to disarm principalities, wrestle with and win power over spiritual wickedness in high places. You, the individual capable of praying through Holy Spirit, moving in the realm of the spirit; are capable of pulling down strongholds. Being born again of Holy Spirit enables you!

Should you decide now to become a born again believer, please believe in your heart that Jesus was born of The Spirit, died on the cross and was raised from the dead for you to enjoy the transformation of being born again of The Spirit! I encourage you to take the time now to accomplish this beautiful birth...

Now that we have a view of who and whose we are, let us take a look at the meaning of pray, prayer and praying.

4

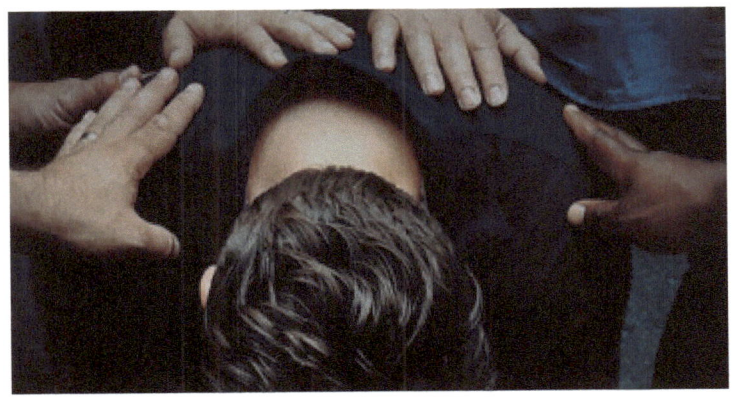

PRAY

We will study the meaning of this word from both the Old and New Testaments along with a few examples of their meanings. Each meaning has one or more scriptures supporting it.

OLD TESTAMENT [Listed 245 times]

577 - Onna = I ask you!, O! Seek forgiveness.

2470 - Hala = Faint, in need of direction.

2603 - Hanan= Repentance, have mercy, take pity.

4994 - Na = I beg you! Now!

6419 -Palal = Justification, good reasoning.

7592 – Sa al = Request on behalf of others.

7878 - Siah = Call upon, complain.

NEW TESTAMENT [Listed 68 times]

1189 - Deomai = Making request.

2065 - Erotao= To urge.

2172 - Euchomai= Pray for; wish for.

870 - Parakaleo= To ask, plead; to comfort, encourage.

336- Proseuchomai= Pray earnestly.

Now let us put together what we have accumulated from the Old and New Testaments regarding the word, "Pray."

We can pray when in need of Onnna [forgiveness], Hala [direction], Hanan [repentance]. It is comforting knowing I can pray, Na [having an urgent need], Palal [for justification], and Sa Al [on behalf of others]. It is good knowing we are able to Siah [complain] and not have our words repeated in gossip!

The New Testament reveals we can Deomai [make a request], Erotao [urge the Lord to move on our behalf, Euchomai [wish for something specific], Parakaleo [plead for comfort and encouragement], and Proseuchomai [we can pray intensely]. All of these are biblically correct methods to pray!

We can see through scripture to pray is a conversation from ones heart to our heavenly Father. We, the body of Christ have the privilege to pray. We are assured due to Jesus giving His life for us and we living our lives for Him, our prayers are heard and, answered. [Isaiah 65:22-24]

The Old Testament way to pray was much different than the New Testament. We observe prophets in the Old Testament having the privilege of knowing God spiritually and being an instrument used mightily. Reason being, at that time Holy Spirit was not available to everyone.

In the Old Testament to pray was almost as if the people were asking God for a rabbit to be taken out of a hat! Request were being made with little remorse. People feared God and followed the law according to their interpretation and, when it suited them. Because the God of Abraham, Isaac and Jacob and the God of Moses was all powerful the people were keeping the law out of fear, not love. Eventually the people were just going through the motions.

Isaiah 29: 13

"Therefore the Lord said: 'In as much as these people draw near with their mouths And honor Me with their lips, But have removed their hearts far from Me and their fear toward Me is taught by the commandment of men.'"

6

Jeremiah 31: 31-33

"Behold the days are coming says the LORD, when I will make a new covenant with the house of Israel and with the house of Judah—[32] not according to the covenant that I made with their fathers in the day that I took them by the hand to lead them by the hand out of the land of Egypt, My covenant which they broke though I was a husband to them, says the LORD. [33] But this is the covenant that I will make with the house of Israel, after those days, says the LORD: I will put My law in their minds, and write it on their hearts; and I will be their GOD , and they shall be My people."

Sweep Over  Your Heart

It is important to always prepare our heart before we pray. To sweep over our heart entails examining ourselves, our motives and attitude before engaging in prayer.

Matthew chapter 6, verses 5-8 instructs us on how to be prepared to pray so our prayers will be heard by our Father. Notice the text is in red, denoting Jesus is speaking and teaching us. It reads as follows:

"And when you pray, you shall not be like the hypocrites. For they love to pray standing in the synagogues and on the corners of the streets, that they may be seen by men. Assuredly, I say to you, they have their reward. [6] But you, when you pray, go into your room, and when you have shut your door, pray to your Father who is in the secret place; and your Father who sees in secret will reward you openly. [7] And when you pray, do not use vain repetitions as the heathen do. For they think that they will be heard for their many words. [8] Therefore do not be like them. For your Father knows the things you have need of before you ask Him."

Here Jesus is explaining to us when we pray, we are not to be hypocritical. We do not pray only to be seen by people and have them impressed. Jesus is instructing us to "check our motive!" When we pray openly, we are to make sure our motivation to pray is not tainted.

Share a few practical ways you can immediately begin to sweep your heart.

_____

_____

_____

_____

_____

PRAYER

Any word with over a hundred examples in scripture of the meaning, deserves in-depth study. We will look into scripture at the meanings for the word, prayer and peek into the dimensions.

OLD TESTAMENT [Listed 83 times]

3908 - Lahas = Charming, a whisper.

8605 - Pilla = A plea, petition.

NEW TESTAMENT [Listed 31 times]

1162 – Deesis = A request.

2171 – Euche = Intercession.

4335 – Proseuche = A position of prayer.

Let us connect all of the meanings of "Prayer" together.

We see the Old Testament Lahas, revealing the word "charming" as a description of prayer. The scripture in Isaiah reveals when we are being chastised or disciplined, we often resist. Somewhat like a child being spanked and moves around to avoid the spanking! There are some circumstances in our life that will cause us to finally become agreeable. A prayer whispered due to the weight or sincerity of the situation we are having to face; and would rather avoid. We have wrestled, cried, hollered and now, 'Lord, whatever you want me to do…' Even a whisper is considered prayer.

Isaiah 26: 16 [Message Bible]

"O GOD, they begged you for help when they were in trouble, when your discipline was so heavy they could barely whisper a prayer."

The Old Testament definition for Pilla; a plea, a petition is slightly different from the definition of pray, due to the fact this plea is in the form of a request being made in an urgent and emotional manner. We see David praying emotional, urgent prayers numerous times when his life was being threatened.

In the New Testament the word Deesis, has the meaning of a request, a petition; however this request comes from a different perspective. We no longer pray to The God of Moses, Who requires an act of contrition in the form of a sacrifice. Now, in the New Testament, repentance confirms our relationship with Christ. Our request and petitions offered in prayer is fueled by faith.

The word Euche: An interview is generally done face to face for the purpose of consolidating facts to determine if the request made should be honored. In intercession we go to our Father on behalf of others and, it is also the faith of the intercessor measured and accounted for when considering the request. This has been done countless times by parents for children. Intercession will be discussed in detail in a later segment.

Proseuche: A position of prayer is not limited to a physical position. The words, By prayer, indicates the approach to take. Holy Spirit grants us an assurance heavenly Father is in control of all things. Paul is encouraging us to be spiritually minded. Anxiousness may arise in us however, being in the position of prayer will invite thanksgiving and peace.

Having explored pray and prayer we see the many proportions and facets to pray and prayer. We have glimpsed into the dimensions of prayer. The importance of getting into The Word cannot be stressed enough. As we grow in our relationship with Holy Spirit, our prayer life will increase. We will actually experience the various dimensions in prayer and glorify our Lord for every encounter!

The disciples had not witnessed the demonstration of answered prayer until Jesus walked with them. Until Jesus' ministry most prayer had become reduced to techniques and forms of manipulation. Prayers were being made to idols that were made by the very hands praying to it. The gods were categorized according to whatever the need. There were those who attended the synagogues and street corners who were religious and prayed with hidden agendas.

Jesus' model prayer is framework for us to use. Direct prayer up to our heavenly Father, honoring Him for Who He is, then welcome His will. Voice your petition agreeing to keep your heart free of unforgiveness, nor allow any obstructions to hinder His will. When Jesus walked the earth having a relationship with heavenly Father was rarely considered during prayer. Jesus willingly giving His life for our ransom, becoming The Lamb Of God; enable our relationship.

Linking pray with prayer allows us to scratch the surface on the elements of prayer.

PRAYING

This is the last word we will look into the meanings of on the topic of prayer. It is of importance because of the examples we have in the scripture. The New Testament has the word listed fourteen times along with examples. We have covered their meanings in pray and prayer. The Old Testament has the word praying listed six times also with scriptures revealing examples. One scripture we have not previously observed for this word is found in the Old Testament. Let's take a look.

OLD TESTAMENT

1156 – Be'a' = To ask for, request; when petitioning deity.

This definition example is found in Daniel chapter 6, verse 11; "Then these men assembled, and found Daniel praying and making supplication before his God." Praying is the actual act of pray and prayer. This biblical meaning for praying; Be' a [asking for, making a request; petitioning deity] is stressing importance on who is being petitioned. Daniel stood out in his day and time because Daniel made the choice to live his life for The Most High God. We can relate. In this day and time we stand out as we live for Christ.

Daniel 6: 10

"Now when Daniel knew the writing was signed, he went home. And in his upper room, with his windows open toward Jerusalem, he knelt down on his knees three times that day, and prayed and gave thanks before his GOD, as was his custom since early days."

11

Daniel petitioned God with his body turned toward where he knew his God to dwell. Daniel understood trusting in God was no option; it was an absolute! Consider Daniel having heard of the miracle shared by Shadrach, Meshach and Abednego being spared in the fire. Daniel humbly submitted his petition to whom he knew was his help.

We have sixty-six books declaring the wonderful works of our GOD! Praying should become automatic for us. Dialogue with Holy Spirit, having a prayer-life must, absolutely be done with a clean heart otherwise the prayers will not be heard.

Isaiah 1: 15,16 [NLV]

"When you lift up your hands in prayer, I will not look. Though you offer many prayers, I will not listen. For your hands are covered with the blood of innocent victims. [16] 'Wash yourselves and be clean! Get your sins out of my sight. Give up your evil ways.'"

Evaluating what we have covered

Examining the thread in Pray, Prayer and Praying forms a pattern; praying becomes second nature to us who are born-again. Depending on where we are spiritually in our relationship with Christ; a novice, utilizing training wheels or having a seasoned rapport. Wherever we find ourselves, what dimension or level of prayer, we need to keep our hearts and minds pure. Our heavenly Father hears us and is examining our heart.

Having a relationship with someone, we spend time with them, we make time to get to know them. The Bible is Gods' resume' so spend time in The Word. Enhance rightly dividing The Word, converse with Holy Spirit daily and grow in understanding.

Take time to reflect on the following questions.

How can I improve my prayer life and strengthen my spiritual relationship?

_____

_____

_____

What steps must I implement to become accountable?

_____

_____

_____

This next session will continue to focus on the introduction to prayer with attention to the times and types of prayer. We will also explore the dimensions of prayer and identify one biblical skill we can incorporate into our study time.

Prayer Times

Prayer times are times we pray specific, targeted prayer. We will look only into three types of prayer including personal, family and the body of Christ.

Let us begin with personal prayer times where we take a good look into a mirror.

Personal prayer time is when you share your moods, fears, hurts, disappointments and how grateful you are for having God's love even when He knows everything about you. For the born-again believer personal prayer time that is coupled with studying The Word will provoke transformation.

John 14: 15-17

"If you love Me, keep My commandments. [16] And I will pray the Father, and He will give you another Helper, that He may abide with you forever- [17] the Spirit of truth, whom the world cannot receive, because it neither sees Him nor knows Him; but you know Him, because He dwells with you and will be in you."

When we love someone, we want to spend time getting to know them. Our love for Jesus giving His life in exchange for ours, while we were yet in our sin; produces a desire in us to live a life pleasing to Him. Holy Spirit dwells in us to help us live as Jesus commanded.

Our personal prayer time is when we have transparent conversations with Holy Spirit.

Allotting time each day for personal prayer time is great! Some choose to spend devotional time as soon as they arise, before any distractions. Some prefer to make prayer and studying scripture the last event of the day, when they are relaxed. There are those who do both. Choose a time preferred by you and maintain your commitment. The principle is to make time investing in your spiritual relationship.

There are occasions we spend time with someone and are not pleased with what we see. For example, we may notice a certain friend gets in touch only when they have a need. After spending time in personal prayer, we may realize we are that friend who only calls

13

on Holy Spirit when in need. Perhaps we realize we do all of the talking...

Please do not feel discouraged if you are that friend. We grow spiritually just as we grow naturally and the more time spent with someone, the closer we become. The more we study The Word and have personal conversations with Holy Spirit, the more of ourselves is revealed.

It is intended for us to see ourselves!

Luke 22: 31-34:

"And the Lord said, 'Simon, Simon! Indeed, Satan has asked for you that he may sift you as wheat. [32] But I have prayed for you, that your faith will not fail; and when you have returned to Me, strengthen your brother.' [33] But he said to him, 'Lord, I am ready to go with You, both to prison and to death.' [34] Then he said, 'I tell you, Peter, the rooster shall not crow this day before you will deny three times that you know Me.'"

Peter spent a lot of time with Jesus and was so sure he would follow Jesus even to death. Jesus knew the plans for Peter and revealed to Peter satan wanted to sift him as wheat and, when Peter returns, he is to strengthen his brother.

Personal prayer time will reveal some things about ourselves and it is not a bad judgement call should we decide to back-off praying when weakness is revealed. As Peter did, take time to process what has been revealed. Remember Jesus is interceding on your behalf and Holy Spirit is also a healer! Allow Him to reveal the root cause of the weakness, surrender to healing and resume your personal prayer time.

Personal prayer time develops over time. When we are a novice, we do all of the talking. As we enter the training wheels stage, we begin asking Holy Spirit to align our responses to The Word. Stepping into the stage of maturity, we wake up each day personally thanking Holy Spirit for keeping us. Personal prayer is vital in our relationship with Holy Spirit. Studying The Word to mirror our life as Christ go hand in hand with personal prayer.

Ephesians 4: 22-24

" That you put off, concerning your former conduct, the old man which grows corrupt according to the deceitful lusts, [23] and be renewed in the spirit of your mind, [24] and that you put on the new man which was created according to God, in true righteousness and holiness."

Take time to examine what your personal prayer time looks like.

<u>List some ways you can improve your personal prayer time and work on accomplishing those improvements.</u>

_____

_____

_____

_____

_____

<u>SCENARIO</u>

As I sat at my desk to turn on my computer, Alison, my boss, Mr. Caldwell's secretary abruptly steps up to me slightly bends over and whispers, "Before you do anything Mr. Caldwell is requesting you in his office." I am reading her face. "Hurry, he is waiting." Alison looks around the room, clears her throat and walks away. Now I am wondering what could Mr. Caldwell want to see me about. As I stand I notice all eyes are on me and I remember my last review not being up to par. Now my heart is racing.

Let's discuss the scenario.

This person dedicates no personal prayer time. How do you think they will respond to being fired?

This person dedicates personal prayer time every morning. How do you think they will respond to being fired.

Prayer Times

This segment we will explore prayer for those we hold close.

This prayer time happens automatically as we grow in the Lord. After we have our personal prayer time we will find ourselves going directly into praying for family, co-workers and neighbors. As we experience the grace and love of God, we want those we hold close to share the same.

Psalm 37: 3-5

"Trust in the LORD, and do good; Dwell in the land and feed on His faithfulness. [4] Delight yourself also in the LORD, and He shall give you the desires of your heart. [5] Commit your way to the LORD, Trust also in Him, And He shall bring it to pass."

David is encouraging us to trust in the Lord. Doing good is allowing Holy Spirit who lives in us to direct us. Doing good is being obedient to His Word.

Delighting ourselves in the Lord is not a directive of works to be completed. We do not check off a list of things to do to give the appearance we are serving the Lord. David is referring to a heartfelt delight. Experiencing pleasure in our surrender and trusting Holy Spirit is not a grievous or coerced experience. This is a process that takes time.

The Lord will give us the desires of our heart. We will not have to aid Him; He will give them to us. No manipulation on our part is needed. The Lord will cause whatever we desire to become His concern. Family members, co-workers and neighbors we interact with daily or on a regular basis; their concerns will become our concerns. We will include those we hold close to us in our prayers.

Here are a few examples of trusting the Lord. Being obedient and delighting oneself in the Lord will cause these very scriptures to come alive in our lives.

Example # 1

In Genesis chapter 47, verses 1-12, we see Joseph informing Pharaoh of his father and brother's arrival in Goshen. The relationship between Joseph and Pharaoh was one built on trust. Pharaoh gave permission for Joseph's family to own the best part of land located in Rameses.

Example # 2

Matthew chapter 1, verses 18-21; Mary was spared being humiliated due to Joseph the man she was to be joined in marriage to, being, "a just man," received a dream informing him not to put Mary away.

Our prayer time including family, co-workers and neighbors are considered appropriate. Some families pray together at appointed times. There are groups of co-workers who create a time of prayer at work to pray for the business and one another's needs. I have known a group of neighbors bind together at a selected time and place to pray for one another. These are all acceptable times to pray for those we hold close.

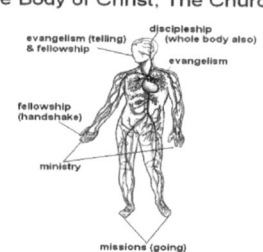

PRESCRIPTION  Times

This last discussion will be on *the Body of Christ.*

A body represents unity in diversity. As we mature spiritually we will include time to pray for the Body of Christ. When we understand Christianity is a body ministry, that understanding will prompt prayer for one another.

Some congregations assemble monthly, quarterly or have a scheduled time of prayer. Department heads may schedule times of prayer for the needs, such as Missions, Outreach and the likes.

Ephesians 4: 16 [HCSB]

"From Him the whole body, fitted and knit together by every supporting ligament, promotes the growth of the body for building up itself in love by the power working of each individual part."

Just as the natural body experience malfunction and the whole body is affected; it is likewise concerning the Body of Christ. The Body of Christ encounters resistance from the spirit realm as well as the natural realm which is cause for praying for one another. Collectively we can pray and witness miracles!

Acts 12: 5; 16

"Peter was therefore kept in prison, but constant prayer was offered to God for him by the church. [16] Now Peter continued knocking; and when they opened the door and saw him, they were astonished."

Prayer Types

In this section we will examine through scripture, the different types of prayer we can offer up.

Keeping in mind conversations [PRAYERS] prompted by situations vary. Depending on who we are praying for is also a variant.

THANKSGIVING

Psalm 92: 1 & 2

"It is good to give thanks to the LORD, And to sing praises to Your name, O Most High; [2] To declare Your lovingkindness in the morning, And your faithfulness every night."

There are times, even weeks, when you just cannot seem to thank God enough! When a victory occurs or a testimony of the wondrous works He has done. When looking back over your life or the life of a loved one, gratefulness engulfs us and we cannot stop thanking Him for the twins! [Grace and Mercy]

There is a song with these lyrics, *"When I think about the goodness of Jesus, and all He has done for me, my soul cries out, hallelujah! Thank God for saving me!"* When we begin recalling the circumstances grace and mercy have brought us through; it is not easy to put a sock in it! You feel like the pink bunny; you can go on, and on.

PRAISE AND WORSHIP

PRAISE

OLD TESTAMENT

1984 – Halal = Give thanks, cheer, extol.

8416 – Thilla = Proclaiming the excellence of a person or thing.

Psalm 146:1,2

"Praise the LORD, O my soul! [2] While I live I will praise the LORD; I will sing praises to my GOD while I have my being."

NEW TESTAMENT

134 – Aineo = Speaking of the excellence of God.

1391 – Doxa = Glory, splendor, brilliance.

5214 – Hymneo = Sing hymns, sing praises.

Luke 18: 42, 43

"Then Jesus said to him, "Receive your sight; your faith has made you well." [43] And immediately he received his sight, and followed Him, glorifying God. And all the people, when they saw it, gave praise to God. "

Praise is an action word. We include sound and/or movement when we praise the Lord. When contemplating on His works, His grace, and His goodness towards us, we can expect some action!

WORSHIP

OLD TESTAMENT

7812 – Saha = To bow down, reverence.

1 Chronicles 16: 29

"Give to the LORD the glory due His name; Bring an offering and come before Him. Oh, worship the LORD in the beauty of holiness!"

NEW TESTAMENT

4352 – Proskyneo = Pay homage show reverence, to kneel down.

John 4: 23

"But the hour is coming, and now is, when the true worshipers will worship the Father in spirit and truth; for the Father is seeking such to worship Him."

Worship is heartfelt. Worship will draw us into the presence of the Lord, and His presence can be felt. Bowing down is effortless when worship engulfs us.

Praise and worship is not limited to happening at a church service. We can devote time during our study and prayer to not ask for anything; just praise Him for Who He Is. Allow worship to fill our hearts.

HEALING [HEAL]

OLD TESTAMENT

7495 – Rapa = To be cured, to repair, recover, made whole.

Jeremiah 30: 17

" 'For I will restore health to you And heal you of your wounds,' Says the LORD, 'because they called you an outcast saying, 'this is Zion: no one seeks her.'"

NEW TESTAMENT

2323 – Therapeuo = To serve, to give help, cured.

2390 – Iaomai = To be healed, freed, make whole.

Matthew 4: 23

"And Jesus went about all Galilee, teaching in their synagogues, preaching the gospel of the kingdom, and healing all kinds of sickness and all kind of disease among the people."

Let us get understanding about this because some of us have been disappointed and wounded due to our prayers for healing not being granted.

A headache is just as important as cancer or Covid-19 when you are in need of a healing. Becoming healed of our past, the costly mistakes that were made; we cry out knowing Holy Spirit is able to heal just as when Jesus walked this earth. We have promises in The Word that our heavenly Father wants what is good for us and we pray reminding Him of what he has told us. Like telling a four-year old you will treat him to ice cream later; every twenty-minutes the four-year old will remind you of what you said you were going to do.

Yet diagnosis of healing is not being seen by doctors, the pain has not subsided, doubt enters our thoughts and unbelief slowly take over. You hear yourself asking, 'Will I [they] ever be healed?'

Therefore, we must have conversations and we must learn to hear Holy Spirit speak. James chapter one, verse five instructs us should we lack wisdom, to ask for it. God will honor His Word. Keep praying!

Care to share a disappointment experience?

_____

_____

_____

_____

FINANCES [MONEY]

OLD TESTAMENT

3701 – Kesep = Silver piece.

Deuteronomy 23: 21-23

"When you make a vow to the LORD your God, you shall not delay to pay it; for the LORD your God will surely require it of you, and it will be sin to you. [22] But if you abstain from vowing, it shall not be sin for you. [23] That which is gone from your lips you shall keep and perform, for you voluntarily vowed to the LORD your God what you have promised with your mouth."

NEW TESTAMENT

5536 – Chrema = Wealth, possessions, riches.

Acts 24: 26

"Meanwhile he also hoped that money would be given him by Paul, that he might release him. Therefore he sent for him more often and conversed with him."

Money is the currency used in our economy and is a necessary commodity that requires us to incorporate discipline. Unhealthy issues that lie in our soul will prompt uncontrollable spending. Praying every month for the rent to be miraculously paid, when there is adequate income is an indication of unhealthy issues.

Ecclesiastes 10:19

"…But money answers everything."

The word, "answers," refers to respond or counter. What we can or cannot participate in is determined by our affordability. We are to manage our money in a wise and mature manner. When we are mature enough to listen during our prayer time for the solution to having lack every month, Holy Spirit will provide the answer.

Luke 16: 1,2,3

"He also said to His disciples; 'There was a certain rich man who had a steward, and an accusation was brought to him that this man was wasting his goods. [2] So he called him and said to him, 'What is this I hear about you? Give an account of your stewardship, for you can no longer be steward.' [3] Then the steward said within himself, 'What shall I do? For my master is taking the stewardship from me. I cannot dig; I am ashamed to beg.'"

The word, "steward," means manager, administrator and trustee. Godly wisdom is necessary when distributing our finances. We are to pray to become good stewards of our finances and be obedient. Not being wise in the past results in mismanaging our money. Being led by Holy Spirit in our spending will not only lead us out of overwhelming debt, it will teach us how to be good stewards.

Haggai 1: 2-11

"Thus speaks the LORD of hosts, saying: 'This people says, The time has not come, the time that the LORD'S house should be built.' [3] Then the word of the LORD came by Haggai the prophet, saying, [4] 'Is it time for you yourselves to dwell in your paneled houses, and this temple to lie in ruins?' [5] Now therefore, thus says the LORD of hosts: 'Consider your ways! [6] You have sown much, and bring in little; You eat, but do not have enough; You drink, but you are not filled with drink; You clothe yourselves, but no one is warm; And he who earns wages, Earns wages to put into a bag with holes.' [7] Thus says the LORD of hosts: Consider your ways! [8] Go up to the mountains and bring wood and build the temple, that I may take pleasure in it and be glorified, says the LORD. [9] You looked for much, but indeed it came to little; and when you brought it home, I blew it away. Why?' says the LORD of hosts. 'Because of My house that is in ruins, while every one of you runs to his own house."

<u>Examine your financial expenditures; which items need to be deleted?</u>

_____

_____

<u>Which items should be paid off first?</u>

James 1:5 "If any of you lack wisdom, let him ask of God, who gives to all liberally and without reproach, and it will be given to him."

_____

25

Prayer Dimensions

We will now examine a few dimensions of prayer.

What do you see in the picture? A duck or rabbit? Once we are born of the spirit it is expected of us to grow. Just as in the natural we experience stages of life; it is also true for spiritual growth as well. As we grow in our spiritual relationship, our prayer life enriches; causing us to experience dimensions of prayer.

The Merriam Webster Dictionary has several definitions for the word, "dimension." The definition we will use to describe prayer dimensions is a level of existence or consciousness.

Hebrews 5: 13,14 [HCSB]

"Now everyone who lives on milk is inexperienced with the message about righteousness, because he is an infant. [14] But solid food is for the mature—for those whose senses have been trained to distinguish between good and evil."

1 Peter 2: 2 [HCSB]

"Like newborn infants, desire the pure spiritual milk, so that you may grow by it for your salvation."

Having a consistent prayer life and studying The Word generates spiritual growth. The Word reveals to us our intended goal to die to self and transform into the image of Christ. Personal prayer reveals our inner man and allows us to determine what areas are a priority for us to work on. As we apply The Word daily in our lives, Holy Spirit leads, guides and directs us as the transformation takes place. This process creates dimensions.

As we grow in the Lord our prayers become less about what we want and become more Word centered. When we enter into a new dimension of prayer, we also experience entering into a deeper dimension of The Word. The Word becomes alive in us!

Example:

As a new Christian my prayers are constantly about the Lord getting my boss off my back. One day my grandmother gets a diagnosis there is a need for her to have surgery. Immediately I shift my prayers to asking the Lord to heal my grandmother. No longer am I concerned about me, myself and I. This shift in my prayer has launched me into another dimension of prayer.

We see the same shifting in life, only we label it stages. When the preschooler enters school, he now has entered the stage of sharing with classmates. It is the same with us experiencing other stages in life naturally, we will also experience spiritually.

We all grow at our own personal pace. Prayers are conversations, conversations from the heart cannot be duplicated by others. We are to love one another, whatever level we may be, and pray for one another to grow in Christ.

Ecclesiastes 11:5

"As you do not know the way of the wind, Or, how the bones grow in her who is with child, So you do not know the works of God who makes everything."

Ephesians 4:14-16

"That we should no longer be children, tossed to and fro carried by every wind of doctrine, by the trickery of men, in the cunning craftiness of deceitful plotting, [15] but, speaking the truth in love, may grow up in all things into Him-Christ- [16] from whom the whole body, joined and knit together by what every joint supplies, according to the effective working by which every part does its share, causes growth in the body for the edifying of itself in love."

<u>Take time to examine what dimension you operate in; where should you be. What steps are needed to take you there.</u>

_____
_____
_____
_____

TOPIC TWO

FAITH DURING PRAYER

This is the first segment on the topic of Faith During Prayer. We will begin with gaining an understanding of the word "faith."

Meaning of Faith

Our heavenly Father's loving kindness is what draws us into a life of completeness; a relationship with Him. As an automobile transports us from one destination to another, our faith is the vehicle moving us toward Jesus, and His lovingkindness is the fuel being used to draw us.

FAITH

OLD TESTAMENT [Listed 2 times]

529 – Emun = To be faithful, trustworthy.

530 – Muna = Faithfulness, steadiness, trustworthiness.

NEW TESTAMENT [Listed 268 times]

3640 – Oligopistos = Of little faith.

4102 – Pistis = Belief, fidelity, trust with an implication that actions based on that trust will follow.

Now we will pour a firm foundation to build on.

Habakkuk 2: 4

"Behold the proud, His soul is not upright in him; But the just shall live by faith."

The Lord is answering Habakkuk as to why God says nothing when the wicked devours a person more righteous than himself. It is interesting how the Lord answers describing the soul of man is not righteous, not honest but, the just shall live by faith.

The word **JUST [6662 – Saddig = upright in accordance with God's standard]**

When reading Habakkuk 2: 4, the question arises, *'what does the soul of a man have to do with faith?'* Here the scripture is being used as an example in the Old Testament's definition of faith. The definition stated; to be faithful, trustworthy and steadiness, were descriptive of the God of Abraham, Isaac, Jacob and Moses.

These adjectives describe how God was known to the people at that time. The people had only an opinion of Gods' faithfulness. Opinions formed from what was told from generation to generation of the miraculous works of God. How God chose their fathers, Abraham Isaac and Jacob and set them apart. They heard of how God spared lives during the Passover and how He brought the Israelites out of Egypt. The God of their fathers was so far from them, they were of the mindset; all they had to do was appease God and avoid His anger.

God had a reputation of being faithful to the Israelites, His chosen people. Somewhat like the reputation He has with us before our becoming born-again. Because our soul is not in accordance with God's standards, our tendency is to think God will only be faithful to those who attends church.

What was your mindset of God before your born-again experience?

Jeremiah 31: 3

"The LORD appeared to us in the past, saying: 'I have loved you with an everlasting love; I have drawn you with unfailing kindness." [NIV]

The New Testament's definition for the word faith is belief, fidelity, trust with an implication on knowing Gods' history, His actions will follow.

Trust and belief in our Savior giving His life for a ransom is being exercised in our heart when we are being drawn to Him. The fact we are born into a world far from being spiritual minded, for us to trust and believe Jesus being born of a virgin, living His life as an example that a godly relationship is possible with the Father and dying for our sins; all of this is "faith" operating in us!

Ephesians 2: 4-10

"But God, who is rich in mercy, because of His great love with which He loved us, [5] even when we were dead in trespasses, made us alive together with Christ [by grace you have been saved], [6] and raised us up together, and made us sit together in the heavenly places in Christ Jesus, [7] that in the ages to come He might show the exceeding riches of His grace in His kindness toward us in Christ Jesus. [8] For by grace you have been saved through faith, and that not of yourselves; it is the gift of God, [9] not of works, lest anyone boast. [10] For we are His workmanship, created in Christ Jesus, for good works, which God created beforehand that we should walk in them."

This explains our salvation is by God's grace and, through our faith. Again, we will use the automobile analogy that if we never start the automobile, it will not transport us. Grace must be accepted through the act of our faith embracing it. And verse ten informs us that God has already predestined us to walk in Christ and perform good works. **So start the car!**

Born into sin, we are influenced to not put our faith in everything we hear. Governed by the influences of this world and experiencing not being told the truth by some, we learn to build defenses. Hearing Jesus loves us so much that He gave His life to pay for our sins can be unbelievable. Holy Spirit ignites our faith by assuring us God's lovingkindness is trustworthy.

Believing that a love is so unconditional and a grace so unbelievable exists, must be spiritual.

There are more than two-hundred examples of faith listed in the New Testament. Here is a scripture that describes what faith is.

Hebrews 11: 1

"Now faith is the substance of things hoped for, the evidence of things not seen."

Faith is the substance of things hoped for. What is the biblical meaning of the word substance in this scripture?

5287 – Hypostasis = Confidence, trust, being sure.

Now let us read the scripture using the meanings of the words faith and substance. "Now belief is the confidence, the trust, the being sure of things hoped for, the evidence of things not seen."

<u>What experiences am I able to label substance?</u>

_____

_____

_____

_____

_____

These are all evidence and testimonies of what faith has produced.

Hebrews 11: 6

" But without faith it is impossible to please Him, for he who comes to God must first believe that He is, and that He is a rewarder of those who seek Him."

We please God placing our faith in Him. We esteem Him over and above all else.

When we ponder this, we can see how we effortlessly believe in so many things. For instance, when we drive a new automobile traveling on the highway transporting us to our destination, we don't even think of the possibility of the car abruptly stopping. Or think about something as simple as sitting in our favorite chair, never giving thought to whether or not the chair will be capable of holding us. Belief is being utilized by us on a daily basis yet, when we apply our faith to spiritual truths, doubt and unbelief surfaces.

What are some other effortless beliefs that we may have?

_____

_____

Prayer coupled with faith in God can change things. It sounds cliché; however it is true. Let us walk through the New Testament and discuss what we see.

Matthew 6: 30

" Now if God so clothes the grass of the field, which today is, and tomorrow is thrown in the oven, will He not much more clothe you, O you of little faith?"

What do you think Jesus is saying to us?

_____

Luke 7: 9 Read 1-9

" When Jesus heard these things He marveled at him, and turned around and said to the crowd that followed Him, 'I say to you I have not found such great faith, not even in Israel!'"

This scripture paints a picture of great faith. We may read this and think it was no big deal. Remember today we have the Bible revealing the wondrous works of God. This event happened before Holy Spirit was available to all. Multitudes of people being fed, healed and forgiven of their sins was unheard of. This man heard of Jesus and knew Jesus was righteous. Yes indeed, the man had great faith.

Matthew 8: 24-26

"And suddenly a great tempest arose on the sea, so that the boat was covered with the waves. But He was asleep. [25] Then His disciples came to Him and woke Him saying, 'Lord, save us! We are perishing!' [26] But He said to them, 'Why are you fearful, O you of little faith?'"

Have you experienced a suddenly situation and had to summons the Lord? Please share.

_____

_____

_____

Mark 5: 34

"And He said to her, 'Daughter, your faith has made you well. Go in peace, and be healed of your affliction.'"

This woman had done all there could be done and yet she was still in need of healing. She heard of Jesus and made sure to get close enough to just touch the hem of His garment. Jesus did not have to lay hands on her, ask if she wanted to be healed, no, this woman ignited her faith and thought no one would know her "belief" was operating.

Luke 17: 19 Read 11-19

" And He said to him, 'Arise, go your way. Your faith has made you well.'"

Jesus was becoming well known for His healing and feeding multitudes. There were ten lepers who noticed Jesus as He was entering a village and they cried out for Jesus to have mercy on them. When Jesus saw the lepers He told them to go show themselves to the priests. As the lepers went, they were cleansed. One of them went back and loudly glorified God and fell on his face at the feet of Jesus thanking Him. After Jesus commented on there being ten cleansed but only one, a foreigner returned to give God glory, Jesus told the Samaritan to go, his faith made him well.

Romans 10:17

" So then faith comes by hearing, and hearing by the word of God."

Understanding why faith is essential during prayer, we can comprehend the importance of developing our faith. Just as we nourish and maintain our physical bodies for growth, we must nourish and maintain our spirit man for growth. This is accomplished by praying, reading, studying, and meditating on The Word. Holy Spirit will give understanding and teach us while we develop in our spiritual knowledge.

Remember one of the New Testament's definition for the word faith is trust with an implication that actions based on that trust will follow!

James 2: 17-20

" Thus also faith by itself, if it does not have works, is dead. [18] But someone will say, 'You have faith, and I have works.' Show me your faith without your works, and I will show you my faith by my works. [19] You believe that there is one God. You do well. Even the demons believe—and tremble! [20] But do you want to know, O foolish man, that faith without works is dead?"

Please share an experience where you had to prove your faith.

_____

_____

_____

_____

_____

Here is a scripture we will use to wrap-up this session.

1 Peter 1: 7

" that the genuineness of your faith being much more precious than gold that perishes, though it is tested by fire, may be found to praise, honor, and glory at the revelation of Jesus Christ."

Do not allow yourself to become overwhelmed by this warning. The same love that drew us to Jesus will keep us. Holy Spirit will remind us what The Word has to say and teach us how to navigate every situation life presents and every fiery dart the enemy sends our way. Faith is so precious and valuable when we exercise our faith. Faith is believing God will reveal His Word and that directs praise, honor and glory to Him.

We have covered the foundation of what faith means. Next, we will examine the importance of faith during prayer.

This session we will examine why faith is essential when we pray. We will also discuss the necessity of being rooted and grounded in our faith.

Importance of Faith
FAITH = BELIEF

Belief, trust, and fidelity are biblical definitions of the word faith. Faith is activated in us when we are drawn by lovingkindness to salvation. Being born of the spirit our faith must be a constant presence as we develop in our spiritual life.

Now let us think of faith or belief as a person Holy Spirit introduced us to. After the introduction, Holy Spirit informs us that faith will now reside in us. Faith will now be known as belief and will become useful as we develop spiritually.

1 John 5: 4,5

"For whatever is born of God overcomes the world. And this is the victory that has overcome the world—our faith. [5] Who is he who overcomes the world, but he who believes that Jesus is the Son of God?"

Overcoming the world is defined as conquering or prevailing over and against the lure of temptations in our surroundings. We are able to overcome the teachings, influences, and observations we have experienced and thought to be the only truth. Now that we are entering into Gods' truth; we need to be taught how to overcome our observations. This process is only done accurately through faith. With so much mind-renewal needed to be done in us, prayer is an absolute must. We need to keep our line of communication open at all times because some situations may require all through the night conversations!

Hebrews chapter eleven list a host of "by faith" references so, let us glance at a few.

"By faith Abraham obeyed when he was called to go out to the place which he would receive as an inheritance. And he went out not knowing where he was going." Verse 8

"By faith Moses, when he was born, was hidden three months by his parents, because they saw he was a beautiful child; and they were not afraid of the king's command."

Verse 23

"By faith the walls of Jericho fell down after they were encircled for seven days. By faith the harlot Rahab did not perish with those who did not believe, when she had received the spies with peace." Verses 30, 31

"Women received their dead raised to life again. Others were tortured, not accepting deliverance, that they might obtain a better resurrection." Verse 35

Belief becomes a permanent resident in us and should be applied during our prayers. Along with belief; hope and love are also present. Yes, Holy Spirit will equip us with all the spiritual necessities we need.

1 Corinthians 13: 13

"And now abide faith, hope, love, these three; but the greatest of these is love."

Exercising our belief promotes growth and development. When our belief increases, we will experience greater dimensions in our prayer life.

Mark 11: 24

" Therefore I say to you, whatever things you ask when you pray, believe that you receive them, and you will have them."

Matthew 9: 28-30a

" And when He had come into the house, the blind men came to Him. And Jesus said to them, 'Do you believe that I am able to do this?' They said to Him, 'Yes, Lord.' [29] Then He touched their eyes, saying, 'According to your faith let it be to you.' [30] And their eyes were opened…"

1 Thessalonians 2: 13

" For this reason we also thank God without ceasing, because when you received the word of God which you heard from us, you welcomed it not as the word of men, but as it is in truth, the word of God, which also effectively works in you who believe."

The word "effectively" biblically means to produce. Once again, we see belief in operation.

Matthew 17: 20 Read 14-21

" So Jesus said to them, 'Because of your unbelief; for assuredly, I say to you, If you have faith as a mustard seed, you will say to this mountain, 'Move from here to there,' and it will move; and nothing will be impossible for you."

We will address the two issues Jesus is teaching in this scripture. The first is about our unbelief. We must strengthen and develop our belief in God. To everything there is a time and a season. Belief is powerful and when our belief gets shaken or bruised, the risk of not applying belief again may overtake us.

Some situations require fasting and praying to gain victory. When we are faced with a principality, fasting may be required to disarm it. Holy Spirit will reveal what weapons are necessary to use for the particular warfare we are fighting against. Remember Holy Spirit has a long resume' of battle victories. Therefore, we place our belief in Him!

The second issue is when we say to the mountain move from here to there. Jesus was using a metaphor. The mountain represents the situation of the sons epilepsy. We are sure to experience mountain-moving situations for which we pray to be moved.

Do you have a mountain-moving experience you wish to share?

_____

_____

Faith is crucial when we pray. Because our belief in God and His capabilities stems from The Word, it is imperative we read, study, and meditate on The Word daily.

BEING ROOTED AND GROUNDED IN FAITH

Matthew 13: 18-23

"Therefore hear the parable of the sower: [19] When anyone hears the word of the kingdom, and does not understand it, then the wicked one comes and snatches away what was sown in his heart. This is he who received seed by the wayside. [20] But he who received the seed on stony places, this is he who hears the word and immediately receives it with joy; [21] yet he has no root in himself, but endures only for a while. For when tribulation or persecution arises because of the word, immediately he stumbles. [22] Now he who received seed among the thorns is he who hears the word and the cares of this world and the deceitfulness of riches choke the word, and he becomes unfruitful. [23] But he who received seed on the good ground is he who hears the word and understands it, who indeed bears fruit and produces some a hundredfold, some sixty, some thirty."

Do you know of anyone who has walked in this parable?

_____

Colossians 2: 6-10

"As you therefore have received Christ Jesus the Lord, so walk in Him, [7] rooted and built up in Him and established in the faith, as you have been taught, abounding in it with thanksgiving. [8] Beware lest anyone cheat you through philosophy and empty deceit, according to the tradition of men, according to the basic principles of the world and not according to Christ. [9] For in Him dwells all the fullness of the Godhead bodily; [10] and you are complete in Him, Who is the head of all principality and power."

What are some ways we can walk in Christ and gain stronger roots?

_____

_____

Walking with Holy Spirit is a complete belief walk. We do not walk by what we see. We know for a fact that through Gods' Word, He is capable of performing the impossible!

Life will bring about challenges.

James 1: 2-8

"My brethren, count it all joy when you fall into various trials, [3] knowing that the testing of your faith produces patience. [4] But let patience have its perfect work, that you may be perfect and complete, lacking nothing. [5] If any of you lacks wisdom, let him ask of God, who gives to all liberally and without reproach, and it will be given to him. [6] But let him ask in faith, with no doubting, for he who doubts is like a wave of the sea driven and tossed by the wind. [7] For let not that man suppose that he will receive anything from the Lord: [8] he is a double-minded man, unstable in all his ways."

Let's break this scripture down and make it personal to gain understanding. We are being warned of various trials that will happen our way. We get it, it is part of life. However, James is instructing us to 'count it all joy!' James is not telling us to find pleasure in trials. Instead of feeling sorry for ourselves, we should continue developing deeper roots of belief.

We learn from experiencing our circumstances that no matter how it looks, our Father is in control. I am His child, and He promised me I will not have more put on me than I am able to bare.

1 Corinthians 10: 13 NLT

" The temptations in your life are no different from what others experience. And God is faithful. He will not allow the temptation to be more than you can stand. When you are tempted, he will show you a way out so that you can endure. "

Because I know this to be true, I put on my garment of praise when I feel heaviness overtaking me.

Isaiah 61: 3

"To console those who mourn in Zion, To give them beauty for ashes, The oil of joy for mourning, The garment of praise for the spirit of heaviness; That they may be called trees of righteousness, The planting of the LORD, that He may be glorified."

My prayer will now be about my gaining strength from Him and trusting that He has everything worked out for my good. I will endure until the end.

Are you noticing how The Word combats every circumstance we face?

Returning to James; we see the deeper roots of belief are also producing the fruits of patience. Patience having its perfect work in me is developing roots of maturity in my spirit man. Yes, I want to jump up and down, scream and even hit someone not wanting to face this trial. But, I also want to grow up and get pass this toddler stage in my walk with The Lord. I pray for strength and in my private prayer time while I am squirming and crying as I faintly allow patience to have its perfect work in me.

I am praying for wisdom, godly wisdom as noted in Solomon's request in the scripture below.

1 Kings 3: 9 NIV

" So give your servant a discerning heart to govern your people and to distinguish between right and wrong. For who is able to govern this great people of yours?"

While reading this scripture, I noticed how God knows every heart involved in the circumstances and works it out for His chosen. This allows my roots to expand and create deeper understanding.

James is encouraging us to exercise our belief without doubting. We should hide The Word in our hearts to resist the winds of doubt. Keeping ourselves steady in The Word, praying constantly for our roots of belief to be deepened.

It is always after the storm or after the test that we gain understanding. We see His wondrous works manifest and we hear many testimonies. It is always then that we see the budding of fruit on the tree revealing our roots of belief. We thank and bless The Lord for His mercy and grace during storms or tests. This is also where we can grade ourselves on how we can improve.

Without faith we cannot please God. Since we are the only creation possessing belief, our enemy wants to steal it from us. Our belief is so important, we must continuously develop our roots.

<u>Give serious thought on ways you can improve developing your faith roots.</u>

This ends our topic on Faith During Prayer. Next we will journey through Authority During Prayer.

TOPIC THREE

AUTHORITY DURING PRAYER

In this lesson we will explore selected scriptures about the authority given to us during prayer. We will also discuss ways to apply the required criteria for establishing your authority during prayer.

YOUR AUTHORITY

OLD TESTAMENT [Listed 2 times]

7235 – Raba = To increase in number, to multiply.

8633 – Toqep = Power, strength.

NEW TESTAMENT [Listed 35 times]

831 – Authenteo = To usurp authority.

1413 – Dynastes = Sovereign, mighty, of great authority.

1849 – Exousia = The right to control or govern, dominion, human or supernatural.

2003 – Epitage = Command, order.

2715 – Katexousiazo = To exercise authority over or upon.

5247 – Hyperoche = Superiority, excellency.

The word "authority" is mentioned more than thirty times in the New Testament! Our focus for this lesson is on the meaning of the word, "Exousia" which is the right to control or govern. Merriam-Webster Dictionary defines Authority as, "The power to influence or command." Other synonyms for authority include power, jurisdiction, and dominance.

The New Testament and dictionary definitions demonstrate how we have the authority to control, govern, take dominion over, and have jurisdiction during prayer.

Jesus, The Word, becoming flesh generated a living template for the born-again believer. We have already shared how Holy Spirit abides in us with belief, hope and love. Now we will gain understanding of the authority we possess by faith and through Holy Spirit.

Luke 10: 1, 9

"After these things the Lord appointed seventy others also, and sent them two by two before His face into every city and place where He Himself was about to go. [9] **"And heal the sick there, and say to them. 'The kingdom of God has come near to you.'"**

The people in the New Testament had heard testimonies of the miraculous works Jesus had performed and now they were about to witness the same works being done by ordinary people. Remember most of the people thought the God of Abraham, Isaac, Jacob, and Moses was a God you did not want to make angry.

Through Jesus the people observed compassion, healing and forgiveness of their sin. The power causing the miracles Jesus performed was being questioned. Now, lay persons, were performing these same acts and, quoting Jesus about the kingdom of heaven.

Luke 10: 17-20

"Then the seventy returned with joy, saying, "Lord, even the demons are subject to us in Your name!" [18] And He said to them, **"I saw Satan fall like lightning from heaven. [19] Behold, I give you authority to trample on serpents and scorpions, and over all the power of the enemy, and nothing shall by any means hurt you. [20] Nevertheless do not rejoice in this, that the spirits are subject to you, but rather rejoice because your names are written in heaven."**

The seventy Jesus appointed returned amazed about how even the demons were obedient to the Name of Jesus! They applied the name of Jesus and saw with their own eyes the authority contained in His name. Jesus used this teachable moment to explain the authority comes from Him. Jesus also revealed to them the greater joy is in having our names written in heaven!

Having our names written in heaven is the result of us being born-again! The fact that Jesus is directing us to put more significance on our relationship with Him is worth our exploring further.

Matthew 7: 21-23

"Not everyone who says to Me, 'Lord, Lord,' shall enter into the kingdom of heaven, but he who does the will of My Father in heaven. [22] Many will say to Me in that day, 'Lord, Lord, have we not prophesied in Your Name, cast out demons in Your Name, and done many wonders in Your Name?' [23] And then I will declare to them, 'I never knew you: depart from Me, you who practice lawlessness!'"

We believe in the power of God, Christ, Holy Spirit… not ourselves! The only Name whereby we can become saved is the Name, Jesus.

Romans 11: 29

"For the gifts and calling of God are without repentance."

Because our gifted abilities and callings are without repentance, praying in the Name of Jesus will always bring results!

Our relationship being unblemished with our Savior is of the utmost importance. We do what pleases Him motivated by our love for Him and the reward of our spending eternity with Him. The authority we possess during prayer is measured by our belief. When we believe our spiritual relationship is on good terms, we are confident and apply authority with no doubt. When we believe our spiritual relationship is not where it could be, we coward down when applying authority.

Romans 2: 14, 15

"For when Gentiles, who do not have the law, by nature do the things in the law, these, although not having the law, are a law to themselves, [15] who show the work of the law written in their hearts, their conscience also bearing witness, and between themselves their thoughts accusing or else excusing them."

This is very crucial and deserves us getting a clear understanding. Paul explains how our spiritual relationship is derived by a conscience decision made by us to be obedient to God's laws and His Word. Our love for the Lamb who sacrificed His life in exchange for ours motivates us to have and keep our spiritual relationship in good standing. Spending time in The Word and prayer encourages us to examine our conscience as to how we are being faithful in our relationship.

44

This explains how someone can apply authority using the name of Jesus yet be out of relationship spiritually by excusing their unfaithfulness. On the other side of that same coin, our spiritual relationship being in good standing is foremost when we strive for obedience to God's law. This is why Jesus cautioned us, *"Nevertheless do not rejoice in this, that the spirits are subject to you, but rather rejoice because your names are written in heaven."*

Let 's say together:

Lord I repent for any unfaithfulness I excused.

Reviewing what Jesus said in Luke 10: 19, "behold, I give you authority… over all the power of the enemy..." These powerful words Jesus spoke to us heightens our confidence when entering into prayer and when we employ authority.

The permission we are granted by Jesus to apply authority during prayer has requirements. We are to arm ourselves with the full armor of God. This is done by daily absorbing scripture and living in obedience. When we put on the armor, we are weighing ourselves down with The Word, and when the winds of the spirit are being blown during the fighting, we are able to withstand the strategies and schemes of the devil. Our opponent is a liar and an accuser. Being forewarned of his tactics, we are fully armed.

Ephesians 6: 10-12 [NLT]

"A final word: Be strong in the Lord and in his mighty power. [11] Put on all of God's armor so that you will be able to stand firm against all strategies of the devil. [12 For we are not fighting against flesh-and-blood enemies, but against evil rulers and authorities of the unseen world, against mighty powers in this dark world, and against evil spirits in the heavenly places."

<u>Criteria We Must Follow</u>

John 15: 9,10 [HCSB]

"As the Father has loved Me, I have also loved you. Remain in My love. [10] If you keep My commands, you will remain in My love, just as I have kept My Father's commands and remain in His love."

Keeping God's commands simply means we are obedient to His Word. Not wanting to become as those we read about in Matthew 7:21; *"Not everyone who says to Me, 'Lord, Lord,' shall enter into the kingdom of heaven, but he who does the will of My Father in heaven."*

We *must* allow The Word to live in us.

TRANSFORMATION

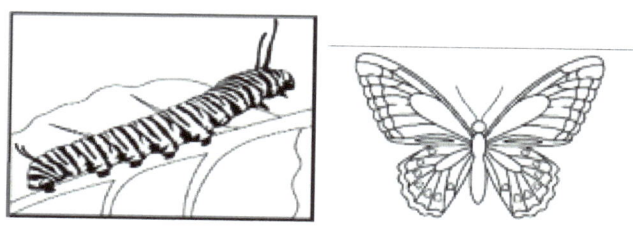

Romans 8: 7, 8 [AMP]

"The mind of the flesh [with its sinful pursuits] is actively hostile to God. It does not submit itself to God's law, since it cannot, [8] and those who are in the flesh [living a life that caters to sinful appetites and impulses] cannot please God."

We not only want to please God; we also want to be transformed into the image of Christ.

Romans 8: 14

"For as many as are led by the Spirit of God, these are the sons of God."

Being led by the spirit is a process. We do not always yield or surrender to the process. Being born into sin and living sinful lives until we are introduced to Christ, our lives were propelled by our soul or flesh. We were carnal-minded and now, we want a spiritual relationship, which means our flesh must be put to death, be done away with. Our old man and his way of processing must now be replaced or renewed by The Word of God. Absorbing scripture and prayer causes transformation in us. Holy Spirit navigates us through this process.

When applying authority in prayer, one of the major strategies the devil will attempt to use against us is our not lining up our life with The Word. When revealed to us an area in our life that needs to be put to death, it is of the utmost importance we work on it. We flinch, squirm and even resist the process of the cutting away of our flesh or carnal self. However, all of this is part of the transformation process.

<u>Lord, help me to surrender to the transformation process.</u>

Romans 12:2 [AMP]

"And do not be conformed to this world [any longer with its superficial values and customs], but be transformed and progressively changed [as you mature spiritually] by the renewing of your mind [focusing on godly values and ethical attitudes], so that you may prove [for yourselves] what the will of God is, that which is good and acceptable and perfect [in His plan and purpose for you]."

Jesus has given us the rights to use His name. Be confident in Him and apply your authority and glorify Him.

Be encouraged and do what must be done to align your life with The Word. No matter how painful or difficult it may be, it is worth every effort!

[Romans 8:18]

 Having authority during prayer is both powerful and valuable. Holy Spirit leads, guides and directs us as we utilize authority during prayer.

There are situations that require assertiveness when we pray and take authority. It is those situations that proper timing must be applied. We will examine how praying The Word will always result in answered prayer and knowing when to be relentless.

Proper Timing When Applying

Authority

Ecclesiastes 3: 1-8 [HCSB]

"There is an occasion for everything, and a time for every activity under heaven: [2] a time to give birth and a time to die, a time to plant and a time to uproot; [3] a time to kill and a time to heal; a time to tear down and a time to build; [4] a time to weep and a time to laugh; a time to mourn and a time to dance; [5] a time to throw stones and a time to gather stones; a time to embrace and a time to avoid embracing; [6] a time to search and a time to count as lost; a time to keep and a time to throw away; [7] a time to tear and a time to sew; a time to be silent and a time to speak; [8] a time to love and a time to hate; a time for war and a time for peace."

This scripture is Solomon expressing what life is—not what we wish it to be. God is the Author of life and His infinite wisdom has appointed times for every occasion. When we are praying specific and direct prayers, we must always inquire of Holy Spirit: "Is this the right time? Are there other factors I need to consider praying about?"

We are reminded in Proverbs 3: 5 and 6; *"Trust in the LORD with all your heart, And lean not on your own understanding; [6] In all your ways acknowledge Him and He shall direct your paths."*

Our Most High God is all wise. He knows the intent of every heart involved in every situation we pray about. His wisdom is matchless! When we pray decreeing His perfect will to be done in regards to a situation; we are applying godly wisdom.

Let's walk through some scriptures confirming the awesome, limitless wisdom of God.

Genesis 1: 1

"In the beginning God created the heavens and the earth."

Genesis 1: 27

"So God created man in His own image; in the image of God He created him; male and "He created them."

Genesis 2: 8; 16-18,21,22

"The LORD God planted a garden eastward in Eden, and there He put man whom He had formed. [16] And the Lord God commanded the man saying, 'Of every tree of the garden you may freely eat; [17] but of the tree of the knowledge of good and evil you shall not eat, for in the day that you eat of it you shall surely die.' "

We see God's wisdom performing all of the necessary preparations before man was created.

Genesis 6: 5-8

"Then the LORD saw that the wickedness of man was great in the earth, and that every intent of the thoughts of his heart was only evil continually. [6] And the LORD was sorry that He had made man on the earth, and He was grieved in His heart. [7] So the LORD said, 'I will destroy man whom I have created from the face of the earth, both man and beast, creeping thing and birds of the air, for I am sorry that I have made them. [8] But Noah found grace in the eyes of the LORD."

Genesis 6: 13,14, 19

"And God said to Noah, 'The end of all flesh has come before Me, for the earth is filled with violence through them; and behold, I will destroy them with the earth. [14] Make yourself an ark of gopherwood; make rooms in the ark, and cover it inside and outside with pitch. [19] And every living thing of all flesh you shall bring two of every sort into the ark, to keep them alive with you; they shall be male and female.' "

Once again, we see God's wisdom at work. When man's will became consumed with not including God in his life; God devised a recovery plan.

Luke 1: 5, 7, 13

"There was in the days of Herod, the king of Judea, a certain priest named Zacharias, of the division of Abijah. His wife was of the daughters of Aaron, and her name was Elizabeth. [7] But they had no child, because Elizabeth was barren, and they were both well advanced in years. [13] But the angel said to him, 'Do not be afraid, Zacharias, for your prayer is heard; and your wife Elizabeth will bear you a son, and you shall call his name John."

Perfect timing! Elizabeth was considered barren, yet we see a glimpse of the depth of God's wisdom at work. John was six months older than his cousin, Jesus. John prepared the way.

John 2: 1-5; 9-11

"On the third day there was a wedding in Cana of Galilee, and the mother of Jesus was there. [2] Now both Jesus and His disciples were invited to the wedding. [3] And when they ran out of wine, the mother of Jesus said to Him, 'They have no wine.' [4] Jesus said to her, 'Woman what does your concern have to do with Me? My hour has not yet come.' [5] His mother said to the servants, 'Whatever He says to you, do it.' [9] When the master of the feast had tasted the water that was made wine, and did not know where it came from (but the servants who had drawn the water knew), the master of the feast called the bridegroom. [10] And he said to him, 'Every man at the beginning sets out the good wine, and when the guests have well dunk, then the inferior. You have kept the good wine until now!' [11] This beginning of signs Jesus did in Cana of Galilee, and manifested His glory; and His disciples believed Him."

Here we witness Jesus performing His first public miracle! Again, His timing is impeccable. At that time everyone in town attended weddings. This time the people talked more about Jesus' miracle than the brides attire on their way home.

Matthew 21: 1-3

"Now when they drew near Jerusalem, and came to Bethphage at Mount of Olives, then Jesus sent two disciples, [2] saying, to them, 'Go into the village opposite you, and immediately you will find a donkey tied, and a colt with her. Loose them and bring them to Me. [3] And if anyone says anything to you, you shall say, The Lord has need of them,' and immediately he will send them.'"

Mark 14: 12-15

"**Now on the first day of Unleavened Bread, when they killed the Passover lamb, His disciples said to Him, 'Where do You want us to go and prepare, that You may eat the Passover?' [13] And He sent out two of His disciples and said to them,** 'Go into the city, and a man will meet you carrying a pitcher of water; follow him. [14] Wherever he goes in, say to the master of the house, 'The Teacher says, 'Where is the guest room in which I may eat the Passover with My disciples?' [15] Then he will show you a large upper room, furnished and prepared; there make ready for us.**"**

Timing is of utmost importance in whatever circumstance we pray about. We must always consider what God has planned and know, and believe His timing is perfect. Every person involved will be affected by the outcome of our prayers and all praise, honor and glory will be unto God alone. Trust Him.

WHO WOULD NOT TRUST A GOD SO LOVING, SO WISE AND SO POWERFUL?

It is common to expect prayer to be answered by how we visualize. However, the answer may manifest differently than anticipated. When this happens, we experience disappointment. When disappointment arrives at your doorstep; this is the perfect time to give a sacrifice of praise to our Most High God. *[Isaiah 61:3 "To console those who mourn in Zion, To give them beauty for ashes, The oil of joy for mourning, The garment of praise for the spirit of heaviness…"]* Because He knows what is best for us and everyone involved. Be reminded of His glorious majesty. Father truly does know best.

There are times we become so emotionally involved when praying, we tend to forget God wants what is best for the situation more than we do! Praying for a child or spouse with an addiction or illness, and watch them progressively turn worse, is very disappointing.

When praying for yourself, you see a lighted path that appears to be perfect yet God is silent. You keep hearing, "Be still and know I AM God."

When warfare has us weeping for months, it does not seem fair. The question we ask is, 'How long Lord must I endure this?'

These are all necessary elements of the process used in developing our prayer life. Yes, even disappointment. The process may cost us a season, but God is getting ready to reward us for life!

Proper timing is God's timing.

<u>Is there a situation you can share where God's timing proved best?</u>

_____

_____

_____ - _____

Isaiah 55: 8,9

*"For My thoughts are not your thoughts, Nor are your ways My ways,' **says the LORD.** [9] 'For as the heavens are higher than the earth, So are My ways higher than your ways, And my thoughts than your thoughts.'"*

The disciples had the mindset that Jesus came to bring His kingdom and reign in their community. Each disciple wanted to share a part in that rulership. We see in Matthew, Mark, Luke, and John, how the disciples were thinking who among themselves who would sit at Jesus right side.

Even after walking with Jesus for years, the disciples thought everything was over when He died. It is the same for us. Even when we have walked with the Lord, had years of prayer conversations, we are still uncertain how our prayers will be answered. Yet, we do know there will be an answer. How God answers will bring glory to Him and most times, leave us awestruck.

We will examine one last scripture about Proper Timing to tie up this session on Authority During Prayer.

Matthew 9: 1-8 [NIV]

"Jesus stepped into a boat, crossed over and came to His own town. [2] Some men brought to Him a paralytic, lying on a mat. When Jesus saw their faith, He said to the paralytic, 'Take heart, son, your sins are forgiven.' [3] At this, some of the teachers of the law said to themselves, 'This fellow is blaspheming!' [4] Knowing their thoughts, Jesus said, 'Why do you entertain evil thoughts in your hearts? [5] Which is easier to say, 'Your sins are forgiven,' or to say, 'Get up and walk?' [6] But so that you may

know that the Son of Man has authority on earth to forgive sins...' Then He said to the paralytic, 'Get up, take your mat and go home.' [7] And the man got up and went home. [8] When the crowd saw this, they were filled with awe; and they praised God, who had given such authority to men."

Let's look at verse two where the men brought the paralytic to the house where Jesus was. We can assume they believed there was a chance their friend could be healed. We covered previously how belief is the vehicle moving us to Jesus. In Mark 2:4, this same incident is being described in more detail. The men actually took roofing tiles off the house to lower their friend directly in front of Jesus. Was their belief moving or what!

Also we see Jesus saying to the sick man his sins are forgiven. Only Holy Spirit knows all things! Jesus knew this man was actually sin sick! God knows every intent of our hearts. When we take authority over a situation in prayer, we must remember Holy Spirit knows exactly what the root problem is. So, we must be in agreement with God's perfect timing knowing He is working on every issue in need of being repaired!

Verse four of Matthew nine reveals Jesus pinpointing the motives of the critics when they entertained evil thoughts. Remember these were learned men of the law who were more concerned about traditions being followed than being in the presence of their Savior. Nope! That is not how we do things here!

Verse eight in Matthew nine reveals that God being magnified in and through us is what our born-again lifestyle is all about. Prayer is life changing and we are walking, breathing testimonies of God's grace and love. Exercise the authority given to you with confidence allowing Holy Spirit to work on every heart involved. As a result, you will be blessed and see yourself mature in The Word.

We will always learn and experience new dimensions of prayer and be blessed by the encounters. Remember this is our lifestyle now that we walk with Holy Spirit daily. We will not always get a targeted bullseye; we Learn from the mistakes. Humble yourself and share with others who have made praying a lifestyle. All the glory belongs to Him!

This ends our segment on Authority During Prayer. Next we will begin with Intercessory During Prayer.

TOPIC FOUR

INTERCESSORY DURING PRAYER

In this segment, we will define Intercessory, and review the job description of an intercessor.

According to The Merriam Webster Dictionary, the word Intercessory is defined as: *the act of interceding. A prayer, petition, or entreaty in favor of another;* intercession. Although the word intercessory is not in The Strong's Exhaustive Concordance, these words are listed: intercede, interceded, intercession, intercessions, and intercessor.

We will look into the Old and New Testaments for the biblical definitions of *intercede, interceded, and intercessions.*

INTERCEDE

OLD TESTAMENT [12 times]

2470 – Hala = To implore, to seek favor.

6279 – Atar = To pray, be moved by an entreaty.

6293 – Paga = Plead with, come betwixt.

6419 – Palal = To mediate, intervene.

NEW TESTAMENT [3 times]

2065 – Erotao = To urge, to beseech.

3870 – Parakaleo = To ask, beg, plead.

All of these words imply an appeal or request on behalf of someone other than ourselves. To intercede is to make a plea on behalf of another. Let us see what the Old Testament teaches us about intercede.

Exodus 8: 8,9

"Then Pharaoh called for Moses and Aaron, and said, 'Entreat the LORD that He may take away the frogs from me and from my people; and I will let the people go, that they may sacrifice to the LORD.' [9] And Moses said to Pharaoh, 'Accept the honor of saying when I shall intercede for you, for your servants, and for your people, to destroy the frogs from you and your houses, that they may remain in the river only.'"

Exodus 8:27,28

We will go three days journey into the wilderness and sacrifice to the LORD our God as He will command us. [28] So Pharaoh said, 'I will let you go, that you may sacrifice to the LORD your God in the wilderness; only you shall not go very far away. Intercede for me."

The frogs had overtaken Pharaoh's house, bedroom and his bed. Frogs were in the houses of Pharaoh's servants and were even being found in their ovens! Pharaoh refused to let the people go that they could serve the LORD. With the hardness of his heart, Pharaoh had the audacity to ask Moses and Aaron to 'entreat' the LORD on his behalf! Exodus eight, verse twenty-eight allows us to see Pharaoh is only letting the people go for his benefit; being interceded for. These scriptures reveal how an un-believer will petition for prayer to those who have a relationship with the Lord.

INTERCEDED

OLD TESTAMENT [15 times]

2589 – Hannot =Verbal entreat.

2603 – Hanan = Have mercy, take pity

NEW TESTAMENT [3 times]

2138 – Eupeihes = Submissive, obedient, compliant.

3868 – Paraiteomai = To request, to beg.

The word entreated means plead with, especially in order to persuade; ask urgently. Here are a few examples we find in scripture where God answered prayer that were petitioned by someone else.

Genesis 25: 21

"Now Isaac pleaded with the LORD for his wife, because she was barren; and the LORD granted his plea, and Rebekah his wife conceived."

2 Chronicles 33:12,13

"Now when he was in affliction, he implored the LORD his God, and humbled himself greatly before the God of his fathers. [13] and prayed to Him; and He received his entreaty, heard his supplication, and brought him back to Jerusalem into his kingdom. Then Manasseh knew that the LORD was God."

These are powerful examples of what interceded looks like for us. Be inspired, place your hope in The Word, knowing God answers prayer. How much more are we inspired today knowing Holy Spirit dwells in us! We are the humbled, the honored and the privileged for having Holy Spirit dwell in us.

INTERCESSIONS

NEW TESTAMENT [Once]

1783 – Enteuxis= Prayer.

1 Timothy 2:1,2 NIV

"I urge, then, first of all, that petitions, prayers, intercession and thanksgiving be made for all people- [2] for kings and all those in authority, that we may live peaceful and quiet lives marked by godliness and holiness."

Paul covers all perspectives for us to include in our prayers. Praying for all people to come to the knowledge of Jesus Christ as Lord and Savior is of the utmost importance. Praying for kings and all those in authority covers our whole governing body. Praying for our local, city and statewide legislators, and workers to have peaceful and quiet lives marked by godliness and holiness should be included in intercession.

Now we will look into the Old and New Testaments for the biblical definitions of intercession and intercessor.

We are created with different type personalities and this is due to our heavenly Father being all wise! He knows the persons who will intercede for our government with immense passion. He also knows the persons who will pray tirelessly for our children. When each intercessor prays specific, targeted prayers, and heartfelt concerned prayers; all things are covered.

INTERCESSION

OLD TESTAMENT [listed 4 times]

6293 - Paga = To strike, to touch, plead with, intervene, cause encounter, come between, pray.

NEW TESTAMENT [listed 5 times]

1793 – Entynchano = To appeal, petition.

5241 – Hyperentynchano = To intercede, make intercession.

Intercession is when we pray for others. Intercession is an unselfish act of prayer. Intercession is motivated by compassion. Let us look into the Old Testament and to get an understanding of what intercession was.

Isaiah 53:12

"Therefore I will divide Him a portion with the great, And He shall divide the spoil with the strong, Because He poured out His soul unto death, And He was numbered with the transgressors, And He bore the sin of many, And made intercession for the transgressors."

This scripture is referring to Jesus, our Lord and Savior. He who became flesh and poured His soul out and died for us. Jesus giving His life allowing us to be able to experience life with a spiritual personal relationship. We see Jesus going further after death and resurrection; now making intercession for us. Pleading and intervening on our behalf to become strengthened, and remain faithful to the love relationship made available to us through Him.

Jeremiah 7:16

"Therefore do not pray for this people, nor lift up a cry or prayer for them, nor make intercession to Me, for I will not hear you."

Here we see God has had it with Israel, His chosen people. Israel has disobeyed the God who brought them out of Egypt and has refused to follow His instructions. We see here that there is an instance where God can become so fed-up, He wants to hear nothing from His rebellious children. If you are a parent, you can relate, especially during the 'pre-teen and the teen stage!'

Jeremiah 27:18

"But if they are prophets, and if the word of the LORD is with them, let them now make intercession to the LORD of host, that the vessels which are left in the house of the king of Judah, and at Jerusalem, do not go to Babylon."

Jeremiah brings attention to , 'if the word of the LORD is with them.' In the Old Testament times, the prophets were appointed to intercede on behalf of the people. Today, due to the love Jesus carried out for us on the cross, we have Holy Spirit living in us enabling us with the privilege each day to experience a one-on-one conversation. Keep your relationship in good standing and the Word of the Lord will be with you.

Now we will walk over to the New Testament to take a look into intercession.

Romans 8:26,27;34

"Likewise the Spirit also helps in our weaknesses. For we do not know what we should pray for as we ought, but the Spirit Himself makes intercession for us with groanings which cannot be uttered. [27] Now He who searches the hearts knows what the mind of the spirit is, because He makes intercession for the saints according to the will of God. [34] Who is he who condemns? It is Christ who died, and furthermore is also risen, who is even at the right hand of God, who also makes intercession for us."

Due to us housing a soul, where our personalities and five senses live, we are prone to revert to our carnal or not spiritual thinking. We are limited in comprehending beyond our experiences. Holy Spirit is all knowing and pleads on our behalf for our strength and knowledge of God's will to become increased. God's Word is His will.

Jesus clothed Himself in flesh, walked the earth and endured what we endure. He felt what we feel. Jesus is qualified and capable of making an appeal to God on our behalf. He is well acquainted with our sorrows, our pain, and our struggles. Who can be a better intercessor!

Hebrews 7:25

"Therefore He is also able to save to the uttermost those who come to God through Him, since He always lives to make intercession for them."

Through the death of our Savior, we are permitted to approach God with repentance and be given the opportunity to become born-again. Jesus becoming The Lamb that was slain for us, qualifies Him to plead, petition and make an appeal on our behalf. Oh! What love…

Having the knowledge of unconditional love bestowed upon us by Jesus, we form a love relationship with our Savior. Our love for Jesus is our motivation to be and remain faithful in our love relationship.

By now we have established a consistent personal prayer time and find ourselves praying more for others. We have moved into the dimension of intercessor. We will now take a look at the biblical definition of intercessor and will review the job description.

INTERCESSOR:

<u>*Definition*</u>

OLD TESTAMENT [Once]

6293 –Paga = To strike, touch, intercede for.

Isiah 59:14-17 NIV

"So justice is driven back, and righteousness stands at a distance; truth has stumbled in the streets, honesty cannot enter. [15] Truth is nowhere to be found, and he whoever shuns evil becomes a prey. The LORD looked and was displeased that there was no justice. [16] He saw that there was no one, he was appalled that there was no one to intervene; so his own arm worked salvation for him, and his own righteousness sustained him. [17] He put on righteousness as his breastplate, and the helmet of salvation on his head; he put on the garments of vengeance and wrapped himself in zeal as in a cloak."

This scripture describes Christ as our redemption and He is our example. We can apply this same characteristics upon ourselves. This scripture is also parallel to Ephesians six.

Ephesians 6: 10-18 NIV

"Finally, be strong in the Lord and in his mighty power. [11] Put on the full armor of God so that you can take your stand against the devil's schemes. [12] For our struggle is not against flesh and blood, but against the rulers, against the authorities, against the powers of this dark world and against the spiritual forces of evil in the heavenly realms. [13] therefore put on the full armor of God, so that when the day of evil comes, you may be able to stand your ground, and after you have done everything, to stand. [14] Stand firm then, with the belt of truth buckled around your waist, with the breastplate of righteousness in place, [15] and with your feet fitted with the readiness that comes from the gospel of peace. [16] In addition to all this, take up the shield of faith, with which you can extinguish all the flaming arrows of the evil one. [17] Take the helmet of salvation and the sword of the Spirit, which is the word of God. [18] And pray in the Spirit on all occasions with all kinds of prayers and requests. With this in mind, be alert and always keep on praying for all the saints."

We are fortunate to have a love so strong and compassionate bestowed upon us. Our heavenly Father has equipped us with everything we will need to combat and conquer our enemy, the devil. We have daily conversations with Holy Spirit, hide The Word in our hearts, and we are capable of extinguishing every fiery, flaming arrow thrown at us. That is the confidence we hold onto when we intercede with the full armor of God!

Having The Word in us and speaking, decreeing, and declaring what The Word says is our security. So now that we know how we fight and win in prayer, let's take a look into who this job is for.

Intercessor:

Job Description

Prayer is a method us born-again believers apply to cause change. Our prayers aligned with God's Word will bring results that glorifies God and build our confidence in The Word. Sometimes an occasion will arise causing us to apply force and Holy Spirit holds the highest record of TKO's and we are on His team!

Collectively, intercessors do damage to the works of the devil. The devil wants to steal, kill and destroy. However we come right behind him just as Jesus did in the garden of Gethsemane and heal, repair and restore during intercession. As we mature in intercession, we will be alerted before damage is done and prevent the damage from being done.

Intercession allows Holy Spirit to work signs and wonders and miracles! The very courses of life are being changed according to the will of The Most High God! Intercessors, get in position and let's pray The Word and do some damage to the devils works!

Intercessor: DNA

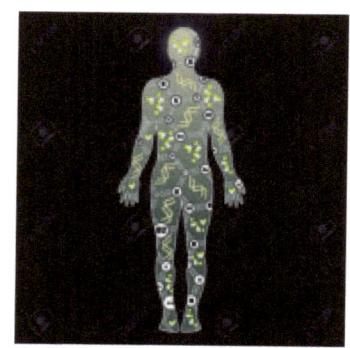

While growing up did you ever come across a game in progress and joined the losing team? Ahh, give yourself a DNA match. How about overhearing a conversation of someone being put down and you get so upset, feeling the person being discussed is being victimized. Ahh, give yourself another DNA match. This one is a bit tricky; do you find yourself wide awake in the middle of the night and absolutely cannot get back to sleep? You may think you have consumed too much caffeine. No, caffeine is not the issue…You have earned another DNA match!

Do you have an intercession testimony ?

_____

_____

_____

Prayer is drawing you captive! Holy Spirit wants to share conversation with you. Listen and align what you hear to The Word. Intercession has requested your prayers. There are times and seasons when intercession will invade your thoughts for a particular person, place or matter.

Remember we are privileged to both realms, the spiritual and the natural. You fit the job description of an intercessor. You are now equipped with Holy Spirit to intercede when summonsed.

Our next and last segment will cover Maintaining Confidence During Prayer.

Maintaining Confidence

In this last segment we will examine how to *Maintain Confidence During Prayer.*

 We have examined prayer being conversations, the importance of faith abiding in us, the authority we have in the name of Jesus, and the effectiveness of intercession. To develop and experience dimensions of prayer, there is a prerequisite we must adhere to: Keeping Our Fountain Clean!

We previously discussed sweeping over our heart making sure our motive and attitude remains untainted. Now, we will explore how keeping our fountain [which is our mouth] clean, and be aligned with maintaining confidence during prayer.

Intercession involves pulling down strongholds and decreeing The Word over circumstances. When we bind the enemy and take authority over the works of destruction, we are fighting in the spirit.

Being born into sin, we learn to fight physically and verbally. Now we are born-again of the spirit and our fight is spiritual not physical. Our weapons are not carnal but are mighty through God. Holy Spirit is capable of targeting and dismantling the origin of whatever we are being challenged with in prayer.

Having utilized our mouths skillfully before our born-again experience, we now must discover how to skillfully utilize The Word... and ***this takes time!***

One of the greatest obstacles in the life of a born-again believer is imperfection. Our mouth or our tongue now becomes our artillery and The Word becomes our weapon of choice.

Revelation 12: 10

"Then I heard a loud voice saying in heaven, 'Now salvation, and strength, and the kingdom of our God, and the power of His Christ have come, for the accuser of our brethren, who accused them before our God day and night, has been cast down.'

Whenever a slip-up with our tongue occurs, our enemy is sure to say to us, "See, you are not qualified to pray nor take authority over anything! You're not even saved!" Our enemy comes at us with accusations and we must repent and counter the enemy with The Word.

Having a cussing tongue before becoming born-again was our weapon most often used to fight with. Being skilled in using our tongue to get people told was our specialty! There are some situations where temptation to cuss will arise due to our pattern of behavior. You are capable of being just as skilled using your tongue now allowing Holy Spirit to teach you! Our tongue is a very powerful weapon and intercessory requires a clean tongue. Do all you can not to yield to the temptation.

James 3: 7-12 [Amplified Bible]

"For every species of beasts and birds, of reptiles and sea creatures, is tamed and has been tamed by the human race. [8] But no one can tame the human tongue; it is a restless evil [undisciplined, unstable], full of deadly poison. [9] With it we bless our Lord and Father, and with it we curse men, who have been made in the likeness of God. [10] Out of the same mouth come both blessing and cursing. These things, my brothers, should not be this way [for we have a moral obligation to speak in a manner that reflects our fear of God and profound respect for His precepts]. [11] Does a spring send out from the same opening both fresh and bitter water? [12] Can a fig tree, my brothers, produce olives, or a grapevine produce figs? Nor can saltwater produce fresh."

Luke 6: 45

"A good man out of the good treasure of his heart brings forth good; and an evil man out of the evil treasure of his heart brings forth evil. For out of the abundance of the heart his mouth speaks."

<u>**Let's examine this statement and compare our pattern of behaviors.**</u>

If you cuss someone out and afterwards intercession is required, the accusation that will come to mind is, "You cussed that person out. Do you really think God is going to hear your prayer? You are a hypocrite!" These occurrences can make you think you are not qualified to pray or intercede. That is far from the truth. Repentance is required.

Handle whatever has happened right after it occurs. Learn from your mistakes and work at not repeating them! Repent and keep your fountain clean. Holy Spirit lives in you and will enable you to combat the enemy's accusations. Practice not holding onto anything that can be used against you. When you know it is time for prayer, get it right. Repent before you leave the house. If something transpires on the way to prayer, repent before you enter into prayer. Disarm the enemy and pray with the authority given to you to shut the enemy down!

If you have a cussing tendency, [**common trait for many Intercessors!**] work on keeping your fountain clean at all times. Transform your mind with The Word. Repent and allow Holy Spirit permission to constantly clean your fountain. The enemy knows your mouth is powerful and will bring accusations against you to hinder you from dismantling his works. It is imperative to get Word in you so that Word is what will spring up when you open your mouth.

Luke 6:44,45 NIV

"Each tree is recognized by its own fruit. People do not pick figs from thornbushes, or grapes from a briers. [45] The good man brings good things out of the good stored up in his heart, and the evil man brings evil things out of the evil stored up in his heart. For out of the overflow of his heart his mouth speaks."

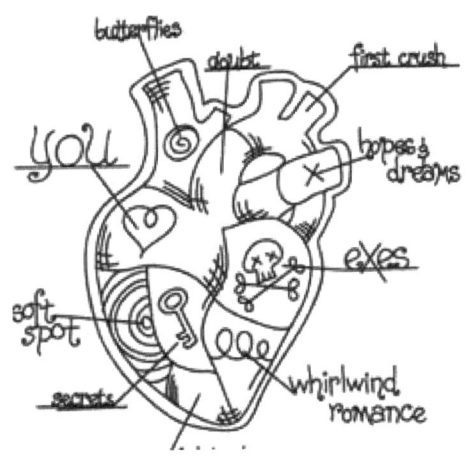

Being born-again we work on developing our inner self, our spiritual self to mirror the image of Christ. Our heart stores our emotions and characteristics, our hurts, our fears and our understanding.

We are now aligning who we were born as, with who we are destined to become in Christ.

When we say something revealing our old man or carnal self, this is notification there is a heart issue in need of attention. Holy Spirit abides in us and is an expert in counseling. Allow Holy Spirit to reveal the root cause of the issue. Then you can receive counsel and total healing.

Isaiah 9:6

"...And His name will be called Wonderful Counselor, Mighty God..."

We must constantly guard our hearts with The Word and our personal prayer time. Praying, speaking and decreeing The Word gives birth to life or death. Yes! We have the power of life and death in our tongues. Take a moment to imagine when the disciples woke Jesus from His sleep on the boat that was being tossed and driven by the waves. Had Jesus spoken disgust from being awaken and not taken authority over the storm and the waves... Well, He is our example. He has given us Holy Spirit and power to overcome which makes deliverance available!

The importance of hiding The Word in our hearts is that it produces a Word declaring tongue.

Hebrews 4:12

"For the word of God is living and powerful, and sharper than any two-edged sword, piercing even to the division of soul and spirit, and of joints and marrow, and is a discerner of the thoughts and intents of the heart. [13] And there is no creature hidden from His sight, but all things are naked and open to the eyes of Him to whom we must give account. "

Proverbs 18:20,21 The Message

"Words satisfy the mind as much as fruit does the stomach; good talk is as gratifying as a good harvest. [21] Words kill, words give life; they're either poison or fruit—you choose."

We have proof that The Word is alive and living. When praying and interceding The Word we can be confident the prayers are being heard and considered. This is why it's vital that we keep our fountain clean!

Let's review some scriptures that prove the power of prayer and intercession.

Revelation 5:8

"Now when He had taken the scroll, the four living creatures and the twenty-four elders fell down before the Lamb, each having a harp, and golden bowls full of incense, which are the prayers of the saints."

Revelation 8:3,4

"Then another angel, having a golden censer, came and stood at the altar. He was given much incense, that he should offer it with the prayers of all the saints upon the golden altar which was before the throne. And the smoke of the incense, with the prayers of the saints, ascended before God from the angel's hand."

Daniel 7:25 KJV

"And he shall speak great words against the most High, and shall wear out the saints of the most High, and think to change times and laws: and they shall be given into his hand until a time and times and the dividing of time."

Do you feel confident in how powerful your prayers are? Do you realize the importance in having a clean fountain? Be encouraged to walk in the calling we have been called to walk in. Let's clean our fountains and walk in confidence knowing our prayers are causing the will of The Most High God to be made manifested.

We will examine one last scripture before closing this segment.

Ephesians 6:10-12

"Finally, my brethren, be strong in the Lord and in the power of His might. [11] Put on the whole armor of God, that you may be able to stand against the wiles of the devil. [12] For we do not wrestle against flesh and blood, but against principalities, against powers, against the rulers of the darkness of this age, against spiritual hosts of wickedness in the heavenly places."

We have examined our fountain also known as the tongue. We gained understanding of the power we possess in prayer. We now have the ability to pray and cause The Word to manifest itself. We are now equipped and confident to apply godly wisdom during intercession.

Intercessors arm yourselves with The Word and do some serious damage to rulers of darkness! Stand against the wiles of the devil. Do what you are called to do during intercession. Take authority over everything out of alignment to The Word of God. Decree and declare the perfect will of the Most High God by the power of the Holy Ghost invested in you. **Be Confident!**

www.ingramcontent.com/pod-product-compliance
Lightning Source LLC
Chambersburg PA
CBHW041429120626
46547CB00002B/148